The Authority of the Believer

a compilation of
The Authority of the Believer and
The Authority of the Intercessor

by

John A. MacMillan

Christian Publications
Camp Hill, Pennsylvania

Christian Publications
3825 Hartzdale Drive
Camp Hill, PA 17011

The mark of 🕈 *vibrant faith*

Library of Congress Catalog Card Number: 80-68065
ISBN: 0-87509-152-0
Compilation of titles formerly published as The Authority of the Believer and The Authority of the Intercessor.
Printed in the United States of America

Contents

Foreword

The rapidly approaching end of the age is witnessing a tremendous increase in the activity of the powers of darkness. Unrest among the nations, more intense than at any previous time in earth's history, is due largely to the stirring up of the ambitions and passions of men, while the spread of an almost wholly secularized education is quietly doing away with the scriptural standards which formerly exerted a restraining influence among the so-called Christian peoples. Our wealth and social culture have not made us thankful to the Giver of all good, but have centered us upon the material things of the world, and have produced a self-sufficiency that quite ignores our dependence upon the Creator of all. Godlessness, which we have condemned so strongly in the Soviet Union, is almost equally as pronounced, though less blatant, in our own land.

These conditions are reacting strongly upon the

great ministry of the Church of Christ, the giving of the gospel to the heathen world. War has closed many doors in foreign lands, and at the same time has cut off financial contributions in not a few countries which formerly took an active interest in missions. More serious still is the attitude of large sections of the church towards the state of the heathen. No longer are these concerned about the lost souls which wander in darkness; their thought is centered on raising their social status and meeting their intellectual and physical needs. They seek, in their own jargon, to "build a better world," but the world they envision is one without a Savior. Christ, in their view, has degenerated into a Superman, an example which in their own feeble strength they seek to follow. To meet the situation, the Church of Christ needs a new conception of prayer. The urgent call is for men and women, wholly yielded to the Lord, whose eyes have been enlightened to see the ministry in the heavenlies to which they have been called. Such believers, whether as intercessors, or as workers at home, or missionaries on the foreign fields, may in union with the great Head of the Body, exercise an authority to which the powers of the air must give place wherever challenged.

The contents of this book first appeared as a series of articles in The Alliance Weekly (now The

Alliance Witness). The first series appeared under the title *The Authority of the Believer*. A second series carried the title *The Authority of the Intercessor*. Both series were subsequently published as pamphlets. This volume combines both booklets since they both deal essentially with the same truth, the authority of the believer.

1

The Authority of the Believer

There are few subjects relating to the Christian life concerning which there is so little exact knowledge as that of the authority of the believer. This is not because such authority is the property only of a few elect souls. On the contrary, it is the possession of every true child of God. It is one of the "all things" received in Christ. Its reception dates from the soul's contact with Calvary.

Probably because of the extreme importance of a correct understanding of its privileges and responsibilities, and because of the power which they confer on a militant believer, the enemy has specially sought to hold back this knowledge from God's people. He has been successful through the employment of the "blinding" tactics which he has found effective in the case of the "lost" and of those who "believe not" (2 Cor. 4:3, 4). For it is strangely true that, although its principles are set forth in a definite way in this epistle to the

Ephesians, there is very little grasp of them by the majority of even spiritual believers.

That there is such authority is recognized, but it is confounded with other aspects of the life of faith, and thereby loses its distinctive value and power. Every doctrine of Scripture, while correlated closely with others of the same class, has features peculiar to itself. Only as these are clearly understood, and held in their right relationship, can there be the fullest benefit from their reception. The constitution and laws of the spiritual world are perfectly orderly and logical, and must be adhered to and carefully obeyed if the desired and promised results are to be gained.

In making this statement it is not intended to suggest that a logical and intelligent mind can of itself grasp spiritual values, or gain possession of spiritual blessings. Were that possible, the deepest phases of the Christian life would be the possession of the most intellectual. Whereas, it is very definitely asserted by the Spirit of God that, in the apprehension of divine truth, "the wisdom of the wise" is destroyed, and "the understanding of the prudent" brought to naught. Thank God, there is an inner spiritual understanding, conferred through the enlightenment of that same Spirit, which enables "the foolish things of the world to confound the wise"—this principle being established by God "that no flesh should glory in his presence."

Wrong Conceptions

The authority of the believer is by some confounded with the fullness of the Spirit. It is taught that the coming of the gracious Spirit of God into the soul in His divine fullness gives authority. But the believer's authority exists before he seeks or realizes in any special way the Spirit's presence. It is certainly true that the fullness of the Spirit empowers and enlightens the believer. By this alone he is enabled to exercise authority. But the fullness is not the source of the authority, but something apart from it.

Nor can authority be regarded as some special gift conferred, whereby the recipient is endued with power, by virtue of which he performs mighty acts, such as the casting out of evil spirits. Discernment of spirits and miraculous powers are mentioned among the *charismata* of the Holy Spirit, but they differ from authority.

By others, the authority of the believer is looked upon as nothing more than prevailing prayer. We have heard men on their knees, when under a special urge, giving thanks to God for the gift of prayer conferred at the time. But, later, there has been no result seen from the agony or enthusiasm of intercession through which they have passed. Personal blessing has resulted from the intense seeking of God's face, but a specific answer to their supplications has not been manifest.

What Authority Is

Let us, first of all, define the difference between "authority" and "power." In the New Testament the translators have not been uniform in the rendering of many words, and these two words have suffered among others. One notable instance is in Luke 10:19 where "power" is twice used although there is a different Greek word in each instance. To have translated the first of these by the English word "authority" would have given a clearer idea of the meaning of the passage. Perhaps our good old English tongue is at times to blame in not providing sufficient synonyms to meet the demands of the original. But a little more uniformity in rendering the same word from the original by the same English equivalent (a thing usually, though not always, possible) would have given greater clearness of understanding although in places it might not have been so euphonious.

One stands at the crossing of two great thoroughfares. Crowds of people are surging by;

multitudes of high-powered vehicles rush along. Suddenly, a man in uniform raises a hand. Instantly, the tide of traffic ceases. He beckons to the waiting hosts on the cross street, and they flow across in an irresistible wave. What is the explanation? The traffic officer has very little "power." His most strenuous efforts could not avail to hold back one of those swiftly passing cars. But he has something far better. He is invested with the "authority" of the corporation whose servant he is. The moving crowds recognize this authority and obey it.

Authority, then, is delegated power. Its value depends upon the force behind the user. There is a story told of the Right Honorable W. E. Gladstone, when he served as Prime Minister of Great Britain. On one occasion, he brought in to Queen Victoria, an important measure for her signature, in order that it might become law. The queen objected to it, and after some discussion, refused to sign. The Minister of the Crown was unusually urgent: "Your Majesty," he said, respectfully but firmly, "you must sign this Bill." She turned on him haughtily: "Sir, I am the Queen of England." Unmoved, the statesman answered quietly: "Your Majesty, I am the *people* of England." After a little thought, she accepted the situation, and affixed her signature to the document.

This story may be apocryphal, but it illustrates the question of authority when two opposing powers are in conflict. The believer, who is fully conscious of divine Power behind him, and of his own authority thereby, can face the enemy without fear or hesitation. Those who confront him bear the specific names of power and authority: "we wrestle not against flesh and blood, but against principalities [*archas*, the first or preeminent ones], against powers [*exousias*, the authorities]." But, behind the "authority" possessed by the believer, there is a "Power" infinitely greater than that which backs his enemies, and which they are compelled to recognize.

The Source of Authority

In the beginning of this article, we made the statement that the soul's authority dates from its contact with Calvary. Let us now point out the meaning and the depth of this truth. When the Lord Jesus, the Captain (*Archegon*, Prince-Leader) of our salvation, was raised from the dead, the act of resurrection was accomplished through "the exceeding greatness of His [God's] power [*dunameos*], to usward who believe, according to that working [*energeian*] of the strength [*kratous*] of His might [*ischuos*]." In this working there was such a putting forth of the divine omnipotence that the Holy Spirit, through the apostle, requires four words of special significance to bring out the thought. We shall not enter into the expressive meaning and grouping of these words further than to say that their combination signifies that behind the fact of the resurrection of the Lord Jesus there lay the mightiest working recorded in the Word of God.

Having been thus raised from among the dead, Christ Jesus was exalted by God to His own right hand in the heavenlies. Then was seen the reason of such mighty working. The resurrection had been opposed by the tremendous "*powers of the air*":—"all principality, and power, and might, and dominion, and every name that is named, not only in this world [*aioni*, age] but also in that which is to come." The evil forces of the "age to come" had been arrayed against the purpose of God. They had, however, been baffled and overthrown, and the risen Lord had been enthroned "far above" them, ruling with the authority of the Most High.

The Conferring of Authority

In calling attention to the "exceeding greatness of his [God's] power," we passed over without comment four words. These are: "*to usward* who believe." All the demonstration of the glory of God, shown in the manifestation of His omnipotence, pointed manward. The cross of Christ, with what it revealed of obedience to God, of atonement for sin, of crushing defeat of the foes of divine authority, shows us a representative Man overcoming for mankind and preparing, through His own incumbency, a throne and a heavenly ministry for those who should overcome through Him.

Observe in this connection the identification of Christ's people with Himself, in this crisis of the resurrection. In the first verse of chapter two, the words read literally: "And you, *being dead* in trespasses and sins," or, perhaps, to bring out better the thought: "And you, *when ye were dead* in trespasses and sins." It will be noticed that we have left out the verb "hath He quickened" which appears in our Bibles. This verb is not in the original; the sentence is incomplete, "being left unfinished," says one expositor, "in the rapidity of dictation." We do not accept this as the explanation of the omission, for we believe that the Holy Spirit so arranged the structure of the whole passage, that the fact might be emphasized that Christ and His people were raised together.

Where, then, do we find the verb that controls this passage? It will be seen in verse 20 of chapter

1: "According to that working of the strength of His might *when He raised HIM from the dead. . .* [then, putting a parenthesis around the words to the end of the chapter]. . .*and YOU when ye were dead.*" The same verb which expresses the reviving of Christ expresses also the reviving of His people. That is to say the very act of God which raised the Lord from among the dead, raised also His body. Head and body are naturally raised together: Christ, the Head; His body, the Church (*ho ekklesia,* the assembly of believers in Him). This is a most important statement, and one of which the definite significance cannot be overestimated.

The same thought, in another form, is developed by the apostle in Romans 6, where the death and resurrection of the Lord Jesus are shown to also include His people. The passage in Romans sets forth (1) the death to sin of the believer with the *crucified* Christ, and (2) the consequent annulling of the power of sin over him though the impartation of the life of the *resurrected* Christ. The believer is thus made a full partaker of Christ's righteousness. But Ephesians lifts (3) the believer with the *ascended* Christ to the heavenlies where he is made a partaker of Christ's throne. In this enthronement, there is an anticipation of that future union in the government of the nations which he shall share with his Lord, ruling them with a rod of iron and breaking them in pieces like a potter's vessel (Rev. 2:26, 27).

The Location of Authority

That there may be no misunderstanding of the Holy Spirit's meaning in this presentation of the truth of the elevation of the Lord's people with their Head, He gives it a second time in chapter 2:4-6. They are made to sit with Christ "in the heavenlies." Christ's session is at the right hand of God. His people, therefore, occupy "with him" the same august position. This honor is not to a chosen few, but is the portion of all those who share the resurrection of the Son of God. It is the birthright of every true believer, of every born-again child of God.

When the Master foregathered with the eleven on the Galilean mountain, at some time during the forty days of His manifestation after His passion, He said to them: "All authority is given unto me in heaven and in earth." His formal assumption of that authority took place when He sat down "on the right hand of the throne of the Majesty in the heavens" (Heb. 8:1). The right hand of the throne of God is the center of power of the whole universe, and the exercising of the power of the throne was committed unto the ascended Lord. He is still there in full possession of His rights, awaiting the Father's time when His enemies shall be made the footstool of His feet.

The elevation of His people with Him to the heavenlies has no other meaning than that they are made sharers, potentially for the present, of the authority which is His. They are made to sit with Him; that is, they share His throne. To share a throne means without question to partake of the authority which it represents. Indeed, they have been thus elevated, in the plan of God, for this very purpose, that they may even now exercise, to the extent of their spiritual apprehension, authority over the powers of the air, and over the conditions which those powers have brought about on the earth and are still creating through their ceaseless manipulations of the minds and circumstances of mankind.

The Rebel Holders of This Authority

It is necessary here to state, what is commonly understood by those who study carefully the Word, that the kingdoms of this world are under the control and leadership of satanic principalities. The great head of these is, in the Gospel of John, three times acknowledged as "Prince of this

World" by our Lord Himself. His asserted claim to the suzerainty of the world kingdoms, made in the presence of the Lord Jesus (Luke 4:6), was not denied by Christ. Although a rebel against the Most High, and now under judgment of dispossession (John 12:31), he is still at large, and as the masses of mankind are also rebels, he maintains over them an unquestioned, because unsuspected, rule, their eyes being blinded to his dominance (2 Cor. 4:4).

The whole rebellious system is divided into heavenly and earthly sections (Isa. 24:21). These are "the host of the high ones on high" (the unseen powers of the air) and "the kings of the earth upon the earth" (the rulers of mankind and their subjects). Both, the prophet tells us, will be judged in that day when "Jehovah cometh forth out of his place to punish the inhabitants of the earth for their iniquity" (Isa. 26:21), and "with his hard and great and strong sword will punish leviathan the swift serpent [the antichrist], and leviathan the crooked serpent [the false prophet]; and he will slay the monster that is in the sea [the dragon]" (Isa. 27:1). Before these acts of judgment occur, the Lord's people will be caught up in the rapture. As Isaiah's eyes were holden to the mystery of the Church, he does not mention it, but he does speak of the hiding of the Jewish remnant from the wrath of the dragon: "Come, my people, enter thou into thy chambers, and shut thy doors about thee; hide thyself for a little moment, until the indignation be overpast" (Isa. 26:20).

The "host of the high ones on high" is carefully divided in our epistle (6:12). There are first the "principalities and powers." The first-named are mighty princes, whose principalities include large areas of the earth, with authority over the nations included in them. The "powers" are difficult to distinguish from them, although attempts have been made to state the difference; they are inferior in position, probably as ministers associated in government.

Following come "the world-rulers of the darkness of this age." This name would suggest a ministry of deception, the keeping in darkness of the minds of men, and especially of the leaders of thought.

Finally, there are "the hosts of wicked spirits in the heavenlies"—an innumerable body of demons, to whose close connection with mankind is due the grosser sins and deceptions, the stirring up of the animal passions, and the incitement to all manner of sensual and sensuous desires. These are the beings that are present in the spiritist seance, impersonating and deceiving people of strong intelligence, like the well-known leaders connected with the cult today.

These beings are also at hand in religious gatherings, and are a source of peculiar danger, especially when the emotions are deeply stirred. Many earnest souls, who have been urged to entire surrender, open their beings with the utmost abandon to whatever spiritual force approaches them, unaware of the peril of so doing. Such yielding often provides an opening for the entrance of demons, who under some pretext gain control of the will. To dislodge them, and to once more free the victim, is usually a very difficult task.

The "kings of the earth upon the earth" comprise human world rulers and their subjects, all unregenerate men. An earthly ruler individually may be a Christian, but he is, by virtue of his office, a member of the great world system which has not yet come under the dominion of the King of kings. All natural men are members by birth also of this system, and so must be "delivered out of the power [exousias, authority] of darkness, and translated into the kingdom of his dear Son" (Col. 1:13).

The seats of authority of these rebellious spiritual rulers are also in the heavenlies. From there they have dominated the human race since its fall. There they will remain until the divine "purpose of the ages" is complete.

2

The Divine Purpose
of the Ages

The "God of the whole earth" does not purpose to tolerate forever this rebellion against His righteousness. "By myself have I sworn, the word is gone forth from my mouth in righteousness, and shall not return, that unto me every knee shall bow, every tongue shall swear." Ere this can be accomplished, the instigators to human rebellion must be cast down. In this regard the divine method is clear. "The powers of the air" are allowed to retain their seats only while their successors are being prepared. God, having redeemed a people and purified them, has introduced them potentially into the heavenlies. When they have approved themselves, they will in actuality take the seats of the "powers of the air," thereby superseding those who have manifested their unfitness and unworthiness.

This purpose, present and future, is very definitely stated in chapter 3:9-11. Here it is revealed as the divine will that "now [nun, the present time] unto the principalities and powers in the heavenly places might be made known *through the church* the manifold wisdom of God." The Church is to be God's instrument in declaring to these rebellious, and now usurping powers, the divine purpose, and in administering their principalities, after they have been unseated and cast down.

This is further declared to be "according to the eternal purpose [*prosethin ton aionon,* the purpose of the ages] which He purposed in Christ Jesus our Lord." That is to say, God, through all the past ages, has had in view this wonderful plan of preparing in Christ Jesus a people, chosen and called and faithful, whom He might place in these heavenly seats to rule through the ages yet to come. It is spoken of, in the verses just preceding, as "the mystery, which for ages hath been hid in God," one phase of this mystery being the wonderful veiling of the deity of the Son of God in our human nature, that we through Him might "become partakers of a divine nature" (2 Pet. 1:4).

This exaltation of the saints and its object were revealed to Daniel in the first of his own great world visions. In verse 22 of chapter 7, after the coming of the Ancient of Days, "judgment was given to the *saints of the most High,** and the time came that the saints possessed the kingdom." A little later (v. 27), we read that "the kingdom and the dominion, and the greatness of the kingdoms *under the whole heaven*, shall be given to the *people of the saints* of the most High." This meaning is clear. The saints of the Most High are the overcoming Church, raised to sit in the heavenlies. Below them, and as objects of their care, are the people of Israel, called here "the people of the saints of the most High." Israel will administer the earthly kingdom, and will be head of the nations. But, overall, will rule the exalted Church, as the executive of God.

The Extent of This Authority

We shall turn again to chapter 1, and consider in detail the powers and things that have been made subject to our Lord, in His exaltation to the Father's right hand. As we meditate on the completeness of His authority, let us remember that He is there as the Representative (Heb. 2:5-9) of redeemed humanity. And "may the eyes of our understanding be enlightened" by the Holy Spirit

---

*The word translated "most High" has the significance of "elevated," and is rendered "high places" in the margin of one edition. This would correspond very closely with the "heavenlies" of our epistle.

so that we may believe, without any doubt or shrinking, that the wisdom and will of the Father have made us sharers of this same authority, and that He verily intends that we should exercise it day by day in growing comprehension and apprehension.

We notice, first of all, that the Risen Christ has been

"Made to Sit"

The act of sitting indicates that, for the time being, certain aspects of His work are in abeyance. Later, the Lord will again "rise up to the prey." But, just now, with "all authority" delivered unto Him, He is awaiting the Father's time, and meanwhile exercising the powers placed in His hands for the working out of the redemption purchased for mankind on Calvary. His session is

"Far Above"

"all principality, and power, and might, and dominion." The great princes and authorities, of whom we have previously spoken, are subject to Him. So are the lesser ones: He is far above all "might" (*dunameos*, a word used usually in the New Testament of spiritual power). This refers to that working of satanic energy which is becoming increasingly manifest, directed as it is against the bodies and minds of the children of God. The inroads that are being made into Christian communities are appalling, but few in the Church are as yet awake to the fact that fresh powers from the unseen world are flooding in upon us. Nor is the cause of this hard to trace. In the parts of the heathen world, where the Word of God energized by the Spirit of God has penetrated, the powers of the air have fallen back. Demon-possession ever retires before an aggressive evangelism, and its manifestations become less frequent. But, in our so-called Christian lands, the authority of the Word is now called in question by the great leaders of the churches, and there are few theological institutions where it is recognized as the very Word of God. In like manner, the Spirit of God is dishonored, firstly, by this very denial of the Word which He has inspired, and secondly, by the disregard paid to His Person and authority. Thus, there is a reversion to heathen conditions spiritually, and as the great agents for the overthrow of demoniacal powers (the Word of God and the Spirit of God) are discredited, these powers are pressing in again upon our country and people. One single evidence of this fact is the tremendous advance that spiritism is making among all

classes; while, as another proof, the very doc-
trines of the Church, depleted, as they are becoming, of their vital spiritual force, are showing un-
doubted marks of those "teachings of demons" of
which the great Apostle bade his hearers beware.

Christ sits also far above all "dominion" (*kurio-
tetos*, lordship). This term is closely allied with
the preceding, much as "principalities and
powers" are grouped together, the second term in
each case signifying similar action on a somewhat
lower plane. In Colossians 1:16, we find
"dominion" connected with "thrones," which
throws light upon the relative term "might." In
this passage and in that quoted from Colossians,
both terms refer directly to spiritual powers,
whereas in 2 Peter 2:10 and Jude 8, the only two
other occasions of the use of the word in the New
Testament, the primary reference is to earthly
dignities.

"In this Age"

He sits far above *"every name that is named, not
only in this world"* (*aion*, age); the great names of
this age are below our Lord. The writer of
Hebrews took pains to point out to Israel that even
Moses was inferior to Messiah (Christ), as a
servant is less than his Master. But what an effort

religious leaders are making today to show that Jesus was only a man, and as such to be ranked with the best men. Over the door of one of the great church buildings of New York, appear figures of some world famous men—such as Emerson, Einstein, Confucius, Buddha, etc., and with them the figure of Christ as one among many! Not so speaks the Spirit of Truth; in His setting forth of the majesty of the Divine Son of God, there are none that can be compared; He is "far above" all. In this continued attempt to exalt humanity, there is to be recognized the working of him who deceived our first parents with the falsehood, "Ye shall be as gods."

"The Age to Come"

"But also in that which is to come." The coming age also yields no name that ranks with that of our Lord. In that age, moreover, the now-dominant spirit-forces shall be bound. Their successors, the glorified Church, shall recognize the preeminence of their exalted King. United with Him, as Head and Body, they will have become manifestly His "fulness." He fills "all in all," but has chosen to do so through His Body. Thus, in the age to come, the members of Christ shall have an active ministry for God throughout the limitless extent of His universe.

"Under His Feet"

"*Hath put all things under his feet.*" The feet are members of the Body. How wonderful to think that the least and lowest members of the Body of the Lord, those who in a sense are the very soles of the feet, are far above all the mighty forces we have been considering. Yet so it is. What need for the Church to awake to an appreciation of her mighty place of privilege. Exalted to rule over the spiritual powers of the air, how often she fails in her ministry of authority, or grovels before them in fear.

"Head over all"

"*Head over all things to the church.*" We have little grasped the force of this marvelous truth. We think of it as if it indicated that Christ was simply in all things and circumstances and places the Church's Head. Let us reverse the words to bring out more clearly their deep significance: "Head to the church over all things." His being Head over all things is for the Church's sake, that the Church, His Body, may be head over all things through Him. We need to sit reverently and long before these mighty truths, that their tremendous meaning may grasp our hearts. In this attitude, the

Spirit of Truth can lift us into their comprehension, which the human mind alone will always fail to compass.

The Operation of God

The argument which we have been following has been thus far centered in the Epistle to the Ephesians. We pass, for a few minutes, to the Epistle to the Colossians, that we may view from a different standpoint how completely this whole matter of the authority of the believer is based on the working of the Father, and how the efficacy of that working depends on the correlated truth of the subjection of Christ to Him. Though coequal with the Father, the Eternal Son accepted a subordinate place, and undertook the task of reconciling, through the blood of His cross, all things unto God (1:20). Having for this purpose yielded Himself under the power of death, He was quickened by "the operation of God" the Father (2:12).

Let us read carefully 2:12-15, noting that the working here indicated is all on the part of God the Father. It is He who (v. 13) quickened the saints together with Christ and forgave their trespasses. It is He who (v. 14) blotted out the adverse decrees of the law, which stood in the way of His people, and nailed the canceled handwriting to the cross of His Son. It is He who (v. 15) spoiled (*ap-ek-dusamenos*, completely stripped) the mighty principalities and powers that had opposed the resurrection of the Lord, and led them captive in triumphal procession in Christ.

A frequent misunderstanding of this passage is that the Lord Jesus "stripped off" from Himself the clustering powers of darkness, overthrowing and putting them to an open shame. But a correct rendering shows clearly that the Agent is God the Father. Of what does He "strip" the powers of the air? Of the authority that had been theirs. Death is the penalty of sin; and when Christ, bearing the burden of the world's guilt, went down to death, they sought to exercise their ancient prerogative and hold Him under its power. But, in the wisdom of the Father, the yielding of the Righteous One to death discharged the long-established bond of the Law. Exultantly, the Father nailed the canceled bond to the cross of His Son; then, "stripping" of their authority the discomfited principalities and powers, He handed this authority to His Son. The "show" (triumphal procession), which the apostle figuratively uses, corresponds to the elevation of the Son above His enemies, mentioned in Ephesians.

Thus, in Colossians there is stressed the Father's working in the active thwarting and overthrowing of the hostile powers, and their subjugation to His Son; while in Ephesians the Son is seen seated above these in all the authority of the Father's throne. The authority of the believer is not taught so fully in Colossians, although the statement is made that, in Him, His people are "complete" (literally, made full). That is to say, through union with Him, they partake of the fulness of the Godhead, which is practically another form of being "blessed with all spiritual blessings."

The Failure of the Church

We saw in a previous section, the Lord as Head over all. His position and power are supreme. Why, then, is there not more manifest progress? Because a head is wholly dependent upon its body for the carrying out of its plan. All the members of its body must be subservient, that, through their coordinated ministry, may be accomplished what is purposed. The Lord Jesus, "Head over all things to the church, which is *his* body," is hindered in His mighty plans and working, because His Body has failed to appreciate the deep meaning of His exaltation, and to respond to the gracious impulses which He is constantly sending for its quickening.

It is a most vital truth of the divine working that

The Word of God

is the pattern by which the ministry of the Church
is framed. The glory of the Body of Christ is the
fact that its members are living members, each
with a personal will. The Holy Spirit comes into
these individual members in order to bring them
into unity with the will and purposes of the Head.
But this is not done through inward impulse alone.
Inward impulse inaugurates obedience towards
the Head, but the renewed mind cannot be fully
instructed save through the Word. Consequently,
it is only as the Word is carefully meditated upon,
understood, and obeyed, that the Head has
freedom of action through its members. How little
the average member feeds, with careful mastica-
tion, upon the Word, most of us know from our
own experience.

The importance of this can be seen by
comparing Ephesians 5:18 ff. with Colossians 3:16
ff. In the first passage, the stirring of the inward
emotions of the heart, with the consequent subjection of believers one to another, in their various
relations, is indicated as the working of

The Spirit of God

in His fulness, but, in the second passage, exactly the same results are pointed out to be the result of the rich indwelling of the Word of Christ. The Word of Christ is the setting forth of His will in a form that is understandable by the renewed mind. But the renewed mind, while understanding the Word, lacks power to perform it. The fulness of the Spirit is the incoming of the Spirit of God to empower the human spirit for the carrying into effect of the accepted will of the Head.

Thus, unless the Word richly indwells for the instruction of the mind, the Spirit of God, although present in His fulness, has nothing to work upon. The impulses of the Head cannot be translated by Him into appropriate action through the Body, but are often like the immature motions of a child. The Head is thereby hindered because the Body has not grown up into the stature of a perfect man. In divine patience the Head waits. Brethren, we are to blame greatly, not only for our own weakness, but also for "the hands that hang down and the palsied knees." God help us to realize this, and to fulfill our ministry through the Word both to others and to the Lord.

3

The Qualifications for Authority

It has been pointed out more than once in this study that the authority of which we are speaking is the portion of every believer. It is not a special gift imparted in answer to prayer, but the inherent right of the child of God because of his elevation with Christ to the right hand of the Father. He has become, through the rich mercy of God, an occupant of the Throne of the Lord, with all that it implies of privilege and responsibility.

This elevation took place potentially at the resurrection of the Lord and because of the believer's inclusion in Him. The elevation is wholly of the wisdom and grace of the Father. We do not "climb the heavenly steeps" by any act of faith or devotion on our part. It is ours simply to recognize the fact of this position, and to take our place in humble acceptance, giving all the glory and honor to God.

Let us recall four words to which mention has

been previously made. They are "*to usward* who believe." In the former reference, we emphasized the first two, pointing out that all the demonstration of the omnipotence of God in Christ pointed manward. We shall now lay stress upon the latter two: "to usward *who believe*." It is not enough that the Divine Fulness outpours unstinted supplies; there must be a receptive heart and attitude on our part. A bottle may be submerged in the waters of a fountain. But, if the cork is not removed, the holder may wait indefinitely, and at last carry it away empty. In accord with this simile, multitudes of truly spiritual believers are, as it were, immersed in the omnipotence of God; it presses them on every side. There is a longing for its experience, and a belief that it should be theirs, and a readiness to receive, these things being the witness of their spirits to the truth which the Holy Ghost has unfolded in the Word. Yet, because their minds have been "holden" as they have read the Word, the simplicity and the glory of this truth have not dawned upon them. Do we not need, indeed, continually to pray with deep heart-humility that "the eyes of our mind may be enlightened"?

Belief

"To usward *who believe*." Few comprehend the

36

primary thought of "belief." It has a twofold meaning, fraught with deep significance. In it are combined two old Anglo-Saxon words: "be," to live or exist; and "lifan," which conveys the thought of accordance. Thus to believe means literally "to live in accordance with" anything. We are accustomed to consider "belief" as simply mental acquiescence with some particular truth. But its root leads us on to action; that which the mind accepts, the will must obey. We do not truly believe, therefore, unless our conviction is manifested in our life. Thus understood, "belief" stands on a par with its great synonym "faith," which, in its deeper sense, means not only to have trust in a person but to manifest that trust by practical committal.

Do we believe that God "hath quickened us together with Christ, and hath raised us up together, and made us sit together in heavenly places in Christ Jesus"? If we do, our reaction to it will be a fervent: "Lord, I accept Thy gracious word. I believe that Thou hast thus wrought for me. In humble faith I do now take my seat in the heavenly places in Christ Jesus at Thy right hand. Teach me how to fulfil this sacred ministry, how to exercise the authority which Thou hast entrusted to me. Train me day by day that I may attain to the full stature of the perfect man in Christ, so that in me Thy purpose of the ages may be fulfilled. Amen."

If we are walking in the spirit, our normal life is in the heavenlies. To secure the consciousness of this, there must be the daily acceptance of the fact. Let us, morning by morning, as one of our first acts of worship, take our seat with Christ (as suggested in the previous paragraph) and return thanks to God for all that it implies. Let us often remind ourselves that we are seated far above all the powers of the air, and that they are in subjection to us. As our faith learns to use the Name and the Authority of Jesus, we shall find the spiritual forces yielding obedience in ways that will surprise us. As we continue to abide closely in Him, our prayers for the advancement of the Kingdom will become less and less the uttering of petitions, and will increasingly manifest the exercise of a spiritual authority that recognizes no national boundaries, but fearlessly binds the forces of darkness in any part of the world.

Humility

While belief thus introduces us to our place of throne-power, only humility will ensure our retaining it. As we compare the abounding grace of God, and our own utter unworthiness, the question arises, Should we need such a warning?

Praise God, it becomes less necessary as the soul grows in grace, and the likeness of the Son increases in us. But we know little of the plague of our own hearts, if we think the danger is ever over. The forces against whom we contend, the principalities and powers, the world rulers of this darkness, the hosts of wicked spirits in the heavenlies, know us far better than we know ourselves. As we attack them, and authority is nought but a long-drawn-out warfare against them, their return stroke is often swift and crushing. With a strategy gained in long experience in spiritual battles, they know that the offensive is their best mode of defense. One of their tested weapons is spiritual pride, and too often it proves effective.

Victory over the powers of the air, from their dread prince downwards, is a demonstrated possibility. But its attainment is alone through the employment of Divine aid. Now, since Eden, man has forgotten that God is essential; through the intervening ages he has constantly sought to show himself self-sufficient. Christ was the first of all our race that ever cast Himself fully upon God. "He trusted in God, let him deliver him," was the sneer of the enemy at Calvary. But at Calvary, the One who had thus fully trusted, could not be delivered. He must go down to death, for the sin question of the world was involved, and the shedding of His precious blood was necessary for atonement. So, "He was crucified through weakness" (2 Cor. 13:4). When this was accomplished, nothing more stood in the way. God raised Him from the dead, stripped His foes of their authority, and set Him on high over them.

With believers, the consuming desire to be independent is something which even the regenerate heart does not fully overcome. Often, just after some signal victory has been gained, there comes the subtle whisper of the enemy, and the overcomer is swiftly shorn of strength through feeling that he is strong.

Boldness

With profound humility, there may go, however, the greatest boldness in the Name. True boldness is faith in full manifestation. When God has spoken, to hold back is not humility but unbelief. In the exercise of authority, there is needed a divine courage that fears nothing but God, and reaches out strong hands to bind and to restrain all that is contrary to Him. But with this courage, there must be a continual and close abiding in God, a spirit that is alert to every urge and check from Him, and a mind that is steeped in the Word of God.

The heavenlies, while the place of "every spiritual blessing" (1:3), are, as well, the place of most intense conflict. Let the believer, whose eyes have been opened to the comprehension of his throne rights in Christ, definitely accept his seat, and begin to exercise the spiritual authority which it confers upon him. He quickly realizes that he is a marked man. Whereas, in his previous ministry, he may have firmly believed in the presence and working of the powers of darkness, and often earnestly prayed against them, there comes now a new consciousness of their existence and imminence. Bitterly they resent and resist his entrance into their domain, and his interference with their workings. Implacable and malignant, they concentrate their hatred against him in an intense warfare, in which there is no discharge. If attacks against his spirit are successfully resisted, assaults may come in mind, or body, or family, or circumstances.

The place of special privilege thus becomes a place of special danger. That there is no truth that encounters such opposition in its presentation is the testimony of those who have brought it forward by voice or pen. We have known of workers, who have taught these truths with acceptance, who have been quite overthrown in spirit or in body, and their ministry rendered useless. Yet, since God Himself, with an eternal purpose in view, has introduced His people into this sphere, we cannot doubt that full provision has been made for their safety.

The Panoply of God

The only place of safety is the occupation of the seat itself. It is "far above" the enemy. If the believer abides stedfastly by faith in this location, he cannot be touched. Consequently the enemy puts forth all his "wiles" to draw him down in spirit, for, once out of his seat, his authority is gone, and he is no longer dangerous, and, further, he is open to attack.

At this point is seen the meaning of the message of chapter 6. To maintain his place against the wiles of the devil, the believer must be constantly arrayed in full armor. The different parts of this armor symbolize certain spiritual attitudes which he must maintain. It is most important to understand that the armor itself when worn constitutes the protection of the believer, and not his activity against the foe. Fully harnessed, he is fully kept, and is unhampered in his ministry of authority. All that he need be concerned about is, like a good soldier, to keep his armor bright and well secured about him.

Let us note briefly the meaning of the various parts of the panoply: no item can be omitted. There is (1) "the girdle of truth," the clear understanding of God's Word, which, like a soldier's belt, holds the rest of the armor in place. (2) "The breastplate of righteousness," not, as often stated, the righteousness of Christ, but rather the active obedience to the Word which he has received. (3) The "feet shod with the preparation of the Gospel of peace," a faithful ministry in the heralding of the Word. (4) "The shield of faith" (*thureos*, the large door-shaped shield covering the whole body), which indicates his complete refuge under the blood of Calvary, where no power of the enemy can penetrate. (5) "The helmet of salvation" (called elsewhere "the hope of salvation," I Thess. 5:8). It is a remarkable fact that the hope of salvation, the coming of the Lord Jesus, is the only helmet that seems able to protect the head in these days of apostasy from the truth. (6) "The sword of the Spirit," which shows the Word of God used in an active sense, even as the "girdle" shows it in a defensive one. (7) "All-prayer," the training of the faculties Godward by constant approach to God.

The emphasis in chapter 6 is laid on victory. Note the following paraphrase which brings out the full force of verse 13: "Wherefore take up with you to the battle the whole armor of God, that you may be able to successfully withstand in the evil day, and having overthrown all foes, to remain unshaken." There is no suggestion of defeat. Secure within his armor, the believer may disregard the enemy, and give his entire attention to the exercise of the ministry to which he has been called.

4

The Practical Exercise of Authority

The believer has now accepted the place of exaltation with his Lord. There has opened for him a life of holiness in the presence of God, and of watchfulness in the presence of the enemy, in a deeper sense than he has known before. His first lesson will be personal. He must learn the significance of the term "Satan" (the Adversary), and come to understand why one of his titles is "Accuser of the brethren." Just as Joshua (Zech. 3:1), when he came to stand before the Angel of Jehovah, found "Satan standing at his right hand to be his adversary," (ASV) so will the spiritually energetic child of God. He will encounter a constant stream of accusations in his own heart. These will trouble him, until he discovers that the purpose of the enemy is to turn him in upon himself, and, through the creating of a consciousness of personal unworthiness, draw him down from the place of perfect faith. He learns to "overcome him by the blood of the Lamb" (Rev. 12:11). That is to say, he presents the Blood as his only answer to these accusations.

But he speedily learns a further use for this divine provision. The Blood represents, not only the cleansing from the guilt and power of sin, but it is also the witness of that overwhelming victory gained at Calvary, by virtue of which the Lord is now seated on high. Once this is grasped, the believer sees that he has not to fight against the foe, but simply to hold over him an already accomplished triumph, the authority of which he shares to the full. Not all at once the full vision comes, but, as he holds his place and exercises his ministry, there will be a gradual perfecting in the heavenly warfare. It will be in his province, as concerns the hosts of darkness, "to bind their kings with chains, and their nobles with fetters of iron," and, in that approaching day of full exaltation in the presence of the King, "to execute upon them the judgment written." Oh, that all God's people might come to the understanding of their high calling, for it is expressly stated: "This honor have *all his saints*" (Ps. 149:8, 9).

The Limitation of Authority

Let it ever be held in mind that the authority

committed to the believer is over the powers of the air, and never over his fellow men or their wills. He is called to bind the unseen forces, but to deliver his brethren. Satan's constant aim is the subjugation of the human will to himself; God's purpose is the full liberation of the will that the freed spirit, through glad acquiescense in the Divine Will, may glorify his Creator. Human control of the will of another, as manifested in hypnotism, etc., is obtained through the use of occult powers latent in the soul, and is as unlawful for the Christian as wizardry and necromancy, which are directly forbidden in the Word of God. Following are a few simple examples of authority in exercise.

Release from Oppression of Body

Just a year prior to this writing, contact was made in a country district with an earnest young pastor and his equally efficient wife—equally efficient in spirit at least, but in body sorely hindered. For long she had suffered from what had been diagnosed as serious heart trouble, and for which medical treatment was being taken. One symptom was the frequent recurrence of severe pains, causing fainting spells. The husband stated that he had several times, on coming into the

47

house, found her lying unconscious on the floor.

While conversing with the wife, she mentioned that her father was a spiritist, and that she had been expert in former days with the planchette. The question was asked: "Is it not probable, sister, that your present physical trouble and your difficulty in receiving healing, is due to the past?" "No," was the serious reply, "for I was never a medium in the ordinary sense. I simply used the planchette," and many interesting and remarkable incidents of its use were narrated. "Nevertheless," the point was pressed, "in using the planchette, your body had to be surrendered to the evil spirit. There is little question in my mind that the difficulty lies there. Your connection with these powers should be acknowledged and confessed. Then a definite stand, in the authority of the Lord, should be taken, absolutely refusing the further working of evil spirits in your body, which has been purchased by the precious blood."

About three weeks after, a letter was received from the sister in question. After the visitor's departure, the light had come; confession had been made; and she and her husband had unitedly refused the further oppression of the enemy. She has never had another attack of heart trouble, and has been blessed in her service greatly.

Some months ago, after a service in one of our cities, two women came asking an interview. The appearance of one gave an immediate understanding of the situation, which was confirmed by conversation. There had been earnest seeking of deep spiritual experience, which was followed by a sudden attack of intense despondency. The attacks persisted, until, after three years, the mind was in complete bondage. All joy had fled, and only a feeble hold of salvation was retained. Suggestions of suicide were frequent, pressing with an urgency that was hard to resist.

The following line of approach was taken, after definitely asserting in prayer the power of the Ascended Lord, and the believer's throne union with Him. "Sister, this trouble is clearly the oppression of evil spirits, which have obtained a hold over you in some manner. These thoughts of self-destruction are directly prompted by him who is a deceiver and a murderer. You are a Christian and united with Christ. This afternoon may be for you, if you will, the last occasion of the manifestation of satanic power." In a simple manner, her place of victory and authority in Christ was shown from the Word. She was urged to take it audibly before those who were witnesses (her sister, a friend, and the speaker). After full assertions of her faith and her acceptance of what Christ had gained and the Father had bestowed, the party kneeled in victorious prayer. As the group arose, one of the friends remarked: "She looks different already." There was a life and animation, most noticeable after the deadness of her previous expression.

A few weeks ago, a letter came: "I feel as if I were saved all over again." Joy and peace had returned; the Holy Spirit had come; and soul-saving work had been granted to her.

Authority over Excessive Anger

"Be ye angry and sin not: let not the sun go down upon your wrath," the apostle charges the readers of the epistle we have been studying; "neither give place to the devil." There is an intimate connection between sinful anger and the prince of evil, and sustained wrath will surely open the door to his entrance. In a certain city two Christian workers, husband and wife, had fallen into the enemy's snare of wrath. One day their quarreling had reached a shameful height, and was attracting attention, as it had done before. The writer and his wife were within hearing, and at prayer. Quietly and definitely they took authority over the spirits of evil who were behind the ostensible cause, and commanded their withdrawal. Almost immediately, the quarreling stopped. As the authority was day by day held and renewed, the spirits were kept in check. Eventually however, the two separated, for they did not seek victory for themselves.

One of the Filipino workers, when a student in the Bible school, was of a very quick and ungovernable temper. This having been stirred up by a trivial matter, he utterly lost control of himself, and speedily became almost insane with rage. The principal and writer stepped into the next apartment, and kneeling down, took the authority of the Lord over the spirits that were working upon him. In a few minutes he was quiet, and it was possible to deal with him.

Similar cases occurred in the Girls' School. On one occasion, after a fight among them, the ringleader was isolated in the office, where she continued shrieking wildly. The writer stepped into the office, sat down, and quietly, and inaudibly exercised the authority of the Lord, commanding the evil spirits to leave the place. The girl instantly ceased, so suddenly that the lady principal asked what had been done to her.

Authority over Fear

In traveling among the islands off the coast of Mindanao, in a native boat, a considerable swell was encountered. The son of the writer began to show fear, which became almost uncontrollable. This was most unusual as he was normally fond of the water, and was an excellent sailor, having frequently traveled up and down the entire China coast, where storms are severe. He begged to be taken ashore; and as the whole affair seemed to be directed against the progress of the evangelistic trip, the writer quietly took the authority of Christ over the spirits of fear and rebuked them, though saying nothing openly. In a very few minutes the lad seemed to change completely, and for the remainder of the journey, lasting several days, there was no further difficulty. The second night after, while in the center of a wide bay, and about twelve miles from shore, a heavy squall was encountered, and an outrigger broke. The danger was imminent, but, though the lad was fully aware of it, and though the waves were washing quite over the boat, he manifested not the slightest shrinking. Other instances of fear, involving older and experienced missionaries, are personally known.

Demon Obsession

Coming down the West River, in the south of China, in 1926, there was a man on board being taken to Hong Kong for mental treatment. He was a foreigner and a member of the customs staff in Wuchow. Early in the morning, he leaped overboard, but was rescued and placed in a cabin on board. A little later he cut his throat from ear to ear. The boat dropped anchor, and native doctors came, sewed, and dressed his wounds. After they had left him, the writer was asked to talk with him. He was lying on the cabin bunk, with his hands secured by a rope. As soon as the cabin was entered, and before any question was asked, he said: "They told me to do it." "Who told you?" "The voices; they are talking to me all the time. They told me to throw myself overboard; and when I was taken from the water, they said there was no hope for me, as I had tried to take my life, and said I must cut my throat." Then, growing excited, he cried, "They are talking to me now; they say I must send you away. Go! Go!" He was quite beside himself. The answer was made: "These are demon voices that speak with you. I am not afraid of them. I have come in here to help you." After prayer, he quieted, and no recurrence of the trouble occurred up to the time he was taken from the boat to the hospital at Hong Kong. He was not delivered, but the trouble was under control while the worker was near. Here it may be said that demons recognize at once anyone who can exercise the authority of the Lord, and they are afraid of him. But full deliverance in such a case as this cannot take place without the consent of the one attacked. Other examples could be given.

Authority over Opposers of the Truth

Previous illustrations are from the personal experience of the writer. The following is by a lady now deceased. In a town in the north of England, great opposition was being manifested to some religious meetings by a group of the rougher sort, stirred by certain communistic leaders. After a short time, the pastor called some of his people together, and asked them to stand with him against the power of the enemy. About a hundred gathered, and after prayer, they definitely repeated with him: "In the name of the Lord Jesus Christ and by His authority we bind the strong man from stirring up these people, and from attacking God's work." A hymn of praise was sung, and the members dispersed. The very next day trouble rose among the leaders of the opposition, some of them left town, and no further hindrance to work was encountered.

Inferences

Such instances as the foregoing might be multi-plied, but these have been selected as illustrating different phases of the question. They are sufficient to show that there are many situations where the direct working of spirits of evil may be inferred. In all such situations, the authority of the Lord is available for the instructed believer. And, where in faith the obedient saint claims his throne rights in Christ, and boldly exerts his authority, the powers of the air will recognize and obey. There may be unwillingness and delay on their part, and time may be required. But, once the word of authority is spoken, it is not necessary to repeat it. The believer must "stand" (6:13), and strengthen himself in God as he waits. He will learn with joy, as did the disciples of old, that "even the demons are subject unto us through thy name."

Apply now these lessons to the great problems of the extension of the Kingdom that face us. *Here is the shortage of funds.* We speak of the financial distress, but is any work of the devil today distressed for funds? A walk on the streets of New York after working hours will speedily give the answer. Satan is choking the channels of Christian benevolence in many and shrewd ways, but he leaves free those which minister to pleasure and sensuality. The writer knows intimately of several cases in widely separated parts of the land where funds are tied up, which, if released, would be instrumental in the advancement of the Gospel.

Here are closed lands. Human governmental authority seems responsible for these. But in the background, there stand the shadowy forms of the great princes (Dan. 10), whose dicta rule the minds and wills of the men whom we see. Afghanistan, Arabia, Tibet, and other lesser areas are thus garrisoned against the entry of the truth. They will thus remain until there rises in the Church believing groups, who shall "agree" that this state of affairs shall no longer continue. And, as such bands, with one accord, exercise a spiritual will of freedom for these lands, saying in the name of the Lord, "This shall not be!" the unseen dominant forces shall be dominant no longer, but shall yield ground, and the barriers shall fall.

Here are hindrances to advance in the field work. Mohammedanism meets us with bigotry and jealousy; paganism with fear and hatred; ignorance binds the heathen mind in darkness that seems impenetrable. Fierce attacks, such as recently occurred in French West Africa, fall upon the workers, and some are cut off. Dissensions rise in the ranks of brethren, and the Spirit of peace withdraws. Behind every such situation the presence of the same malign powers can be assumed. The solution is in their displacement—we alone are to blame that they continue in power.

The same principle is often applicable in personal evangelism. A soul under conviction has great difficulty in grasping the truth, or in yielding to it. His mind is blinded and bound. A quiet attitude of victory over the opposing spirits has often brought swift release. A Filipino student was suspected of lying, but was resolutely standing by his falsehood. Quietly the position was taken: "In the name of the Lord, I rebuke these lying spirits." Suddenly the student broke down, confessed, and wept his way through to victory.

Will it not be worthwhile for the believer to meet in the coming age men and women who have been delivered "out of the snare of the devil," and loosed from varying forms of bondage, because he has stedfastly stood for their deliverance for long periods against the fierce and incessant assaults of these deadly foes?

The Final Outcome of Authority

The question is often asked: Why does God permit this or that condition? Does not the answer lie here? God has planned that man shall, through the out-working of Redemption, regain the place of authority in creation that he has lost. To this end, Christ, having conquered for man, sits as his Representative in the seat destined for him when redemption is fully manifested. In the interim, the wonderful provision exists that man shall be reckoned in Christ, and shall, to the limit of his spiritual understanding and obedience, be endowed with the authority of His name.

Accordingly, God throws upon man the responsibility for the continuance of the conditions which we question. We feel they ought not to be. We realize that they are the working of the enemy. We cry to God to rebuke the enemy, and to alter things. Through the teaching of the Word, He replies: "My children, rebuke the enemy yourselves. The authority over him is yours. Its responsibility I have committed to you. I desire you to learn in these things to prevail. I have purposed a high and holy ministry for you in the coming age. This is for you the time of testing and preparation. Be strong and of a good courage, and none shall be able to stand before you all the days of your life."

Slowly, believers are awaking to their high place of privilege in Christ, and are assuming the responsibilities which it involves. The body of the man-child, who is to rule all nations with a rod of iron, is nearing completion. Born of the Church, but not itself the Church, the body consists of many members with widely differing offices. These members are out of every age and people. On its ascension to the Throne of God, which now potentially it shares, the rebellious powers of the air, which have so long resisted Divine authority, shall be fully and forever dispossessed of their seats to make room for the new incumbents.

Before that event, it is recorded that "the powers of the heavens shall be shaken." The initial tremors of that shaking are now taking place. Every fully yielded heart that crowns Jesus King increases the consternation of the panic-striken hosts. Conscious of their impending overthrow, they are seeking by fierce attacks on every front to hold back the final issue. Now is no time for the Church of Christ to hold back. Let us meet attack by counterattack. Faith is needed, courage, determination, sacrifice. We have these—and more, we have Calvary, with all that it means. Men and women are needed who will meet God in all that He offers, who will take up the cause of the closed lands and reply to the challenge of the great heathen religions by an aggressive warfare in the heavenlies.

"Who is on the Lord's side? Who will face the foe?"

5

The Authority of the Intercessor

So unreasonable to the natural mind seems the proposition of Jehovah to His people (Isa. 45:11) that they should "command" Him concerning the work of His hands, that various alternative readings of the passage have been made with the intent of toning down the apparent extravagance of the divine offer. Men are slow to believe that the Almighty really means exactly what He says. They think it a thing incredible that He should share with human hands the throttle of infinite power. Nor have they the spiritual understanding to comprehend the purpose of the Father to bring those who have been redeemed with the precious blood of His dear Son into living and practical cooperation with that Son in the administration of His kingdom.

The people of Christ are revealed in the New Testament (Eph. 1:23) as "the fulness of him who filleth all in all." They bear a vital relationship to Him as members of His body, through whom His glorious purposes are to be wrought out in eternity. Consequently, it is not a strange thing that, in this present preparatory age, He should make large revelations and offers of His grace, in order that He may test the faith and develop the spiritual powers of those who will be sharers of the authority and ministry of His throne through the coming ages. We need have no fear in accepting the fullest implications of the words above referred to, in spite of the critical attitude of even some devout scholars.

The principle involved is set forth in other places of the Word of God, in different phraseology it may be, but with equal cogency and clarity. Our duty is to draw near with the boldness of faith and in the attitude and readiness of full obedience. Faith will prove a key to unlock every mystery of the truth; obedience will secure our entrance through the door thus opened. In a new and deeper sense we shall discover ourselves to be sons abiding ever in the great house of the Father, partaking of all its relationships and responsibilities. Its many ministries will become vivid as we move about in them, speaking words of authority, and seeing the behests of the Spirit of God, which are uttered through us, carried out to their fulfillment.

In Psalm 20 the coming Messiah is set before us in His human aspect. It is for Him a time of trouble, but the name of the God of Jacob has set Him on high, and divine grace sends forth His help from the sanctuary. His offerings are remembered and accepted before the Most High. Then follows a prophetic petition: "Grant thee according to thine own heart, and fulfill all thy counsel." The desires and purposes of this Chosen Servant of God are promised full accomplishment. All of His heart plans are acceptable to Jehovah; they are in full accord with the divine ideals; therefore, a second assurance is given: "The Lord fulfill all thy petitions."

The One who is thus addressed is the Son of man, the great Representative of our humanity. Through Him the Spirit of God had unhindered liberty in carrying out the divine counsel during all His earthly career. His human will was in constant and perfect alignment with that of the Father in heaven. No shadow ever rose between Him and God save that thick cloud of our sins which enveloped Him on Calvary. At each step of His daily walk He could say, "I do always the things that please him." Because this was true, there was no bar to the granting of the desires of

His heart, or to the fulfillment of His inward counsels.

The deep reality of the union between Christ and His people is but little comprehended by the great majority of believers. It is compared by the Holy Spirit to the relationship of a head to the members of the body over which it is set. Where perfect health prevails, the members are responsive to the slightest impulses of the head. But if disease prevails in any part of the body, there is a lack of full coordination, some member or members being tardy in obedience, or inaccurate in carrying out their rightful functions, or it may be unable to obey at all. The body of Christ differs from the human body in that each member possesses an individual volition which must be surrendered voluntarily to the will of the Head. Much schism, alas, exists also in the body as a whole, and much self-will in the individual member. These things hinder healthy growth and the free outworking of the purposes of Christ. Yet, where any member dwells fully in his place, "holding the head" (Col. 2:19), there is not only full cooperation but also true identity of desire with the Lord, and the Master's promise finds occasion of fulfillment: "If ye abide in me, and my words abide in you, ye shall ask what ye will, and it shall be done unto you" (John 15:7).

Note carefully the significance of the statement, "Ye shall ask *what YE will*." How many believers content themselves with a submissive uttering of the words, "Thy will be done," in all matters which they bring before the Lord. Their spirits assume a passive attitude that accepts anything that comes to them as the will of the Father. This is not scriptural, and it is very far from the desire of God for His children. The Holy Spirit teaches a hearty cooperation rather than mere resignation; an active entering into God's plan instead of a vague yielding to circumstances; a definite claiming and appropriating of the promises which are set before us in the Word, as being the expression of the Father's will for His children. We are to positively will the will of God; to seek it out as He has revealed it; and to maintain our place of quiet assurance before Him until it has been fully accomplished.

Dr. E. E. Helms once told of how he had promised a bicycle to his son. They went out together to inspect the various models, and to make the purchase. The boy led the way to a particular store, and indicated a machine which he said was the one he wanted. His father suggested it might be better to look at some others before finally deciding. But the lad was quite sure as to his own mind. "Father," he said, "I've been scouting round already, and sized them all up, and this is the one I want. I'm going to stay here until I get it." He was successful; and his father in telling the story remarked that if we would take that attitude in our praying there would be fewer unanswered prayers.

That attitude will ensure the carrying out of the promise to the Head: "Jehovah. . .grant thee according to thy heart's desire, and fulfil all thy counsel." The member of the body has come into complete intimacy with the Head; he discerns the purposes of his Lord; through his purposeful petitions, Christ's own heart's desires are fulfilled. Of not a few of the saints this characteristic has been true in a marked degree. It is not the fault of the Head that it cannot be said of all.

The Sharing of Authority

Matthew, in the closing chapter of his Gospel, shows us the King on the mountain in Galilee which He had appointed as the rendezvous for His disciples. He is speaking to the group of followers who surround Him: "All authority hath been given unto me in heaven and in earth." It may seem a strange statement to many Christians, but it is nevertheless a profound spiritual truth that the authority of the risen Head at the right hand of the throne of the Majesty in the heavens, is planned to reach its full development and manifestation through His body. The Son of God became incarnate, not merely that He might save men from their sins, but also that He might bring man to that place of dominion over the works of God which was planned in the counsels of eternity (Ps. 8). Today, the inspired writer tells us (Heb. 2:9), "we see Jesus" holding in trust for redeemed mankind all that the race has lost through sin. Our Lord has Himself taken the Headship, and is forming for Himself a body through which He will fulfill the original divine purpose.

Much of the weakness of the church is due to its failure to understand and appropriate this all-important truth. It is ours, as individual members of the body, to seek that the authority of Christ shall come with full acceptance into our spirits. It is not enough to know and acknowledge that He is our fulness; there must be as well the apprehension of the complementary truth that we are also His fulness (see Eph. 1:23). What an amazing honor and dignity is thus purposed for us: "heirs of God, and joint heirs with Christ" (Rom. 8:17). For the coming of age of the body, and its entrance upon the prepared inheritance, all the rest of God's creation is waiting with earnest expectation.

Serious obstacles often confront the servant of the Lord in his ministry for the bringing in of the kingdom. They seem as deep-rooted as the everlasting hills, and as imposing in their bulk. They block the way to accomplishment of desired ends. They shut out the vision ahead. They balk the disheartened worker with their grim assurance of immobility. They seem to laugh at his discomfiture and to mock his prayers. And, as the months and years pass, and no change is seen in their contour, he comes often to accept them as a necessary evil, and to modify his plans accordingly. Such mountains of difficulty loom up on every foreign field; each home district has its range with impassable serrated peaks towering ahead; few pastorates lack at least a "little hill." They are too varied in their nature to particularize, but they are genuine and heartbreaking hindrances.

Concerning all such, the Master has assured His servants that they need not continue as obstacles to the progress of His work. The question of their removal is one of authority. The command of faith is the divine means of removing them out of the way: "*Ye shall say* unto this mountain, Be thou removed, and be thou cast into the sea; and it shall obey you." The question involved is *not that of an*

imposing faith, but that of an all-sufficient Name.
The worker has no power of himself to accomplish anything, but he is commissioned to wield the power of God. As he speaks to the mountain in the name of Christ, he puts his hand on the dynamic force that controls the universe; heavenly energy is released, and his behest is obeyed.

Authority is not prayer, though the worker who prays can alone exercise authority. Moses cried unto God at the Red Sea (Exod. 14:15 ff.), beseeching Him to work on behalf of His people, only to receive the strong reproof: "Wherefore criest thou unto me? speak unto the children of Israel that they go forward." And, as he lifted his face in amazed protest, because the way ahead was blocked by the impassable waves, Jehovah spoke again: "Lift thou up thy rod, and stretch out thine hand over the sea, *and divide it.*" As the impotent arm of the Lawgiver held over the waters the symbol of the authority of God, there was immediate response, "and the children of Israel went into the midst of the sea upon the dry ground; and the waters [which seemed at first a barrier impossible to overcome] were a wall [of protection] to them on the right hand and on the left."

God delights to delegate His power to men, when He can find believing and obedient servants to accept and exercise it. So, when mountains rise in their way, the Lord commands His disciples to speak unto them and bid them depart into the sea. He gives no instruction to pray, although that is understood. There is essentially the same charge as was given to Moses: "You have asked Me to work; I have granted your request, but I choose to do the work through you; speak to the obstacle before you in my name, and it will obey." As we obediently speak to the mountain before us, there may seem to be no immediate response. But, as day by day, we maintain the attitude of authority, knowing that we are commissioned to use the name of our Lord, there will come a trembling, and a shaking, and removing, and the mountain will slide from its base, and disappear into the sea of forgetfulness.

God is endeavoring to train workers for a future and a mighty ministry of cooperation with His Son. He therefore has here and now conferred on them the privilege of sharing the authority with which Christ was endowed as the Son of man. The burden of responsibility for its acceptance and its exercise lies with the individual believer.

The Binding of the Enemy

A fact that is anew being forced upon the con-sciousness of the Church of Christ is that a great and aggressive warfare is being waged against her by unseen and powerful foes. The Scriptures have long revealed it, but few have given this warfare the attention which it requires. "Our wrestling," the Apostle warns us, "is not against flesh and blood, but against the principalities, against the powers, against the world-rulers of this darkness, against the spiritual hosts of wickedness in the heavenlies" (Eph. 6:12, A.S.V.). In the life of the Christian assembly, in the purity of its doctrine, in the fellowship of its members, and in their individual bodies and circumstances, subtle forces are working with keen understanding and masterful direction. The opposition is veiled, but it is real, and it is sometimes tremendous. Because its source is unrecognized, it is the more effective. The powers of evil are allowed often to have practically free course in groups of believers. Troubles that might be easily overcome, if rightly diagnosed, are laid to other causes, and because the remedy is not applied, the difficulties may increase until the very existence of the congregation is threatened.

In one of the cities of Canada, the pastor of an Alliance Church said to the writer: "There are about four different troubles going on all the time among my people. As soon as I get one straightened out, the devil has another ready to take its place." Answer was made: "Brother, you are right in your diagnosis of the source of your troubles, but you are wrong in your method of meeting them. What you are looking at are the coils of the old serpent through your congregation, and, as you straighten out one kink, you may be sure that another will appear. Leave the coils alone, and go for the head; put your foot on that in the authority of the Lord; recognize the active agency of the enemy and conquer him; the coils will straighten out of themselves if he is dealt with." The same advice will apply in many other places. Let us learn the secret of victory through authority, as well as through prayer, and our churches will come into the place of strength, and be able to take the aggressive against the enemy.

We return to our starting point. The solution of every spiritual problem is to be found in the working of the divine energy. We long for its manifestation, and pray with intensity and with desire that it may be released in our midst. Yet there seems often to be an unaccountable delay that perplexes and discourages. Are we fulfilling the conditions? God is ready to bless, but we fail to provide the channels along which alone can flow His supplies.

It is true also that the Lord is demanding a closer adherence to His appointed methods. As the individual believer matures in the Christian life, he often finds greater difficulty in maintaining spiritual victory. He had expected opposition to decrease, or at least to be more easily overcome. But he discovers that God is laying upon him heavier burdens, and testing him for larger ministries. In like manner, as the age is advancing, the Church is being prepared for the final struggle by being taught lessons of individual responsibility that in the past were the property of advanced saints only. All believers might have known them, for they are revealed in the Word of God, but only the few pressed on to their attainment.

For the greater struggles of our day and the thickening atmosphere into which we are entering, the Church needs intercessors who have learned the secret of taking hold of the power of God, and directing it against the strategic advances of the enemy. She needs those who have understanding of the times to know what ought to be done amid the crashing down of old standards, and the introduction of that which is uncertain and untried.

God is waiting for those whom He can trust and

use, who will have the discernment to foresee His steppings and the faith to command His power. Authoritative intercessors are men and women, whose eyes have been opened to the full knowledge of their place in Christ. To them the Word of God has become a battle chart on which is detailed the plan of campaign of the hosts of the Lord. They realize that they have been appointed by Him for the oversight of certain sections of the advance, and they have humbly accepted His commission. Deeply conscious of their own personal unworthiness and insufficiency, they yet believe God's statement concerning their identification with Christ in His throne power.

Increasingly they realize that heavenly responsibility rests upon them for the carrying forward of the warfare with which they have been charged. Their closet becomes a council chamber from which spiritual commands go forth concerning matters widely varied in character and separated in place. As they speak the word of command, God obeys. His delight is in such co-working. They have caught His thought concerning the method of the advance of His kingdom. Through them He finds it possible to carry forward purposes and to fulfill promises which have been long held back for lack—not of human laborers nor of financial means—but of understanding spiritual fellow laborers.

The Control of Personal Circumstances

In the varied presentations of divine grace and human experience which are set forth in the Book of Psalms, two aspects embrace all others. The first is the *Messianic*, where the psalmist, frequently in his own person, reveals the sufferings and the glory of the incarnate Son of God, whom he recognizes, however, only as the coming King of Israel. The second is the *individual* aspect, in which the relationship of the believing soul to God is portrayed in numerous phases. So fully is the human heart unveiled that David, to whom most of the psalms have been ascribed, has been spoken of by one writer as "not one man, but all mankind's epitome."

The inspiration of the Spirit of God was richly upon all the authors of the Psalms. Each of them knew God, and loved Him with a passion that was, perhaps, not exceeded by any of the saints of this later dispensation. Out of their own knowledge of the inner life they wrote often more wisely than they realized. Without any straining of their words it is possible to find foreshadowings of deep spiritual truths, which in their full development could not be understood till Calvary had come and gone. Comprehension of the mysteries of the heavenly calling comes to men only as they are able to receive them. And, until the work of the Cross was complete, and the Holy Spirit was outpoured, even the most devout of God's true children were not ready for all that has since been revealed to the spiritual minds of the present age.

The Hunger of the Soul

In Psalms 42 and 43 is finely illustrated the thought which has just been stated. There is shown to us the awakening vision of a man whose heart was crying out for knowledge of and fellowship with God. Desire was intensified by the fact that he was in exile. Who he was we may surmise, but his identity matters little. From the "land of Jordan," where the headwaters of that turbulent stream find their sources in the springs of the Hermons, he gazed with inward yearning towards the distant temple. At a former time it had been his privilege to join with the glad throngs of worshippers as they ascended the holy hill of Zion, with songs of rejoicing and praise. Now, isolated amid the solitude of mountain fastnesses and cataracts, he listened with awe to one voice of nature calling unto another of the majesty of the Creator of all, while he himself seemed to be cut off from God and overwhelmed by the waves and billows of the never resting sea of life.

It is sweet to note that, in his remembrance of Jerusalem, he was craving not so much for the ordinances of the sanctuary as for God Himself. It is a precious proof of the reality and the depth of his love that every opposing circumstance but increased his desire for the divine fellowship which he had once enjoyed, which to the pious Israelite found its center of manifestation in the place where God had chosen to reveal Himself. Though the sense of desolation was so great that it seemed to bear him down "as with a sword [a killing or crushing] in his bones," he still believed that the lovingkindness of the Lord was about him "in the daytime" to preserve him from the pursuit of his deadly foes. And then, when the shadows of night fell, and the tabernacle of darkness enfolded him about, there stole into his heart the sweet strains of the songs of Zion mingled with his prayers to the God of his life, and he was soothed and comforted.

The Oppression of the Enemy

His complaint to God concerns spiritual rather than material foes. "Why go I mourning because of the oppression of the enemy," he cries to the most

High, whom he accuses in his depression of having cast him off. The daily reproach of his opponents, "Where is thy God?" is an inward rather than an outward voice, for he was far separated from those who would do harm to him. We are sometimes prone to think that the saints of Old Testament times possessed little clear conception of the powers of the unseen world. But this is a misapprehension on our part. It is true that in the Book of Psalms the emphasis first appears to be laid upon visible and physical foes. These the writer hated "with perfect hatred" (Ps. 139:22), because they were also the enemies of God. But we would be wrong in limiting the thought of the psalmist to what alone could be seen. It will be remembered that Satan is introduced in the very beginning of the Old Testament, and that he appears as the constant adversary of the people of the Lord. The facts also of possession by demons and contact with familiar spirits were well-known and often referred to with reprobation by the prophets and in the Law.

Furthermore, the Book of Job was written long before the time of David, and was unquestionably in his hands and those of the spiritual leaders of Israel. It was doubtless included among the Scriptures in which he meditated with great delight. In this remarkable narrative the veil of the invisible world has been drawn partly aside, and there is given a very startling view of the secret working of the great adversary who had been permitted to bring trouble upon God's champion. We see Satan so concealing his own working that the pious patriarch was actually deceived into believing that he had been set up as a mark for "the arrows of the Almighty." Knowing these facts as they did, it is not too much to claim that David and his fellow saints realized that many at least of the bitter persecutions which they suffered originated from the same dread source that was responsible for the afflictions of Job.

It is a common tendency in the present day to speak of every national calamity as "an act of God," when such should be laid, as surely as in the experience of the patriarch of Uz, at the door of the restless and malignant enemy of mankind. The permission of the Most High has been given, it is true, where such affect the Lord's people, and for this reason the writers of the Old Testament have a tendency to ascribe all things to the direct working of the divine hand. But there is, among the majority of the people of God, an inability to discern in their own sufferings what is the chastening of the Lord, and what is due, in the words of the psalmist, to "the oppression of the enemy."

As a consequence, it is sad to see the numbers of earnest Christians, people like the psalmist with a heart for God, who are being beaten down to the ground, and are unable to rise again. The roll of such is increasing, and it is incumbent on pastors and Christian teachers and workers to appreciate the reality of the danger, and to meet the situation with a keen discernment of its source and a determined will for victory. Unseen wolves are entering, "not sparing the flock," and trained and fearless shepherds are needed, who cannot only face the enemy with understanding and confidence, and can deliver the prey out of his mouth, but who can also repair breaches in the wall of the folds.

6

The Victory of the Believer's Countenance

Three times in the two psalms before us, there occurs a refrain in identical language. It varies somewhat in the Authorized Version, where the translators have employed different words. In the first instance of its use (42:5), the last three words have been attached to the following verse, having probably been so arranged in some manuscript in order to remove what to some scribe seemed an abrupt transition of thought.

The following rendition applies in all three instances (42:5, 11; 43:5). It is quite literal:

> Why art thou cast down, O my soul,
> And why art thou disquieted in me?
> Await God, for I shall yet praise him
> —*The victory of my countenance*—and
> my God.

God is here revealed not merely as the Deliverer of the soul of the psalmist. In the existing circumstances of spiritual oppression and physical depression that would have itself been a splendid achievement of faith. Jehovah is represented in a larger way, as the Giver of victory to the countenance of the psalmist, so that his enemies fled before his face. The Lord had endued His servant with His own authority from on high, so that, as he went forward in the name of God, opposing circumstances should give way and spiritual enemies would flee apace.

This is a New Testament truth in an Old Testament setting. It is one with which every saved and sanctified believer should be familiar. The purpose of the Father provides that each child of His may be a sharer of the throne and the authority of His risen and exalted Son. Over all the power of the enemy this authority extends. It is the believer's right to bind and loose in the name of Him who has appointed him. As the psalm states it, God is Himself the Victory of the believer's countenance, so that he fears neither man nor spirit, nor opposing circumstance.

The Way of the Cross

It is the duty and privilege of every Christian to understand and enter into the divine desire for our perfecting, and to claim the place with Christ, both in His cross and resurrection and ascension, that the Father has appointed. God has reckoned each believer in His Son to have died with Him at Calvary. "Know ye not," demands Paul (Rom. 6:3 ff.), "that so many of us as were baptized into Jesus Christ were baptized into his death?" Alas, it is a truth of which very few who claim the saving grace of our Lord have any practical knowledge, but it is of vital importance. All of our growth into the stature of the risen Son of man depends upon our identification with Him. "Our old man," the apostle goes on to say (v. 6), "was crucified with him, that the body of sin might be annulled" (its power over us destroyed completely and forever). We enter into the experience of this through faith: "Likewise reckon ye also yourselves to be dead indeed unto sin, but alive unto God through Jesus Christ our Lord" (v. 11). Then, as we positively present ourselves unto God as alive from the dead, and withdraw our members from the demands of sin, we shall find ourselves through the action of the Holy Spirit, who carries out within us the action of faith, realizing the truth of the promise (v. 14), "Sin shall not have dominion over you."

The way of the cross is the appointed path to the realization of that experimental sitting with Christ, which the Father has ordained for the believer. Our blessed Lord died at Calvary, and the bands of death being broken, He has been exalted to the right hand of the throne. There is no other way for the disciple than to be as his Lord. It is not a method of fleshly works of self-denial, but the firm belief that God does as He says, as we walk in the light of His truth. Our part is the simple entering by faith into that which has already happened at the cross, the tomb and the resurrection. We yield ourselves unto God that the Spirit may work in us that which He has revealed in His Word as His divine purpose, a purpose which He can only fulfill as we abide in the faith that He is working in us to will and do of His good pleasure. We have died with Christ; we were buried with Him (not in the mere symbolism of water baptism, but in the apprehension of that work of the Spirit which baptism symbolizes); we were raised with Him in His resurrection out of that tomb in which all our sins, and the old man the root of all, were buried; and we have been made to sit with Him in the heavenlies, at the right hand of the Father. It is in the realization which this faith brings that we come to know that the Lord has Himself become the strength of our countenance, as we see a new power working in us and through us in our ministry.

The saint who has learned that the Lord Himself is the victory of his countenance confronts calmly and fearlessly whatever situation may arise, knowing that naught can prevail against the will that is linked with God. A firm and positive refusal that the enemy shall have any right to work in the life, or the body, or the circumstances, will bring the foe to a standstill. And, as this attitude is maintained in quiet faith, a change will come, and the attacks will lose their force. However distressing the assaults it is possible for faith to ask of the inner life, "Why art thou cast down, O my soul, and why art thou disquieted in me?" and to calm itself with the certain assurance, "Await God, for I shall yet praise him—the victory of my countenance—and my God."

The conflicts in our churches, in which neither party will give way, and which lower the spiritual power of the assembly, may be controlled by prayer and authority directed against those evil principalities and powers, whose working foments and continues the trouble. Individual lives, taken in the snare of the devil, depressed and hopeless, may be restored to their place of assurance, and peace, and joy in God. Attacks on physical health, and on social relationships, and

84

on financial matters, may often be traced to unseen workings, and thus overcome in the name of the Lord.

In a wider outlook, the international tumults which threaten the ministry of the gospel through blocking access to needy fields and tying up the sources of financial support, must also yield to the faith that directs the weapons of God against the satanic barriers. The countenance of Joshua was given such victory by the God of Israel that no man was able to stand before his face all the days of his life. Our wrestling, unlike that of Joshua, is not with the seven nations of Canaan, but with their spiritual counterparts. These are the forces that are responsible for every opposing world issue. They, too, shall fall before the Church of Christ, when her people, inspired and energized with a new vision of Calvary, shall rise in the name and authority of the Lord to refuse all interference with her world mission.

Princes with God

It was said of George Muller of Bristol, in his later years, that he bore himself like a prince of God. So confident had his faith become through years of asking and receiving, so intimate was his communion with God from uncounted hours spent in audience with Him, that his countenance and his whole bearing manifested the dignity of a member of the royal household of heaven. The society in which we move inevitably leaves its impress upon us. This is the more true when it demands the putting forth of our highest powers to walk worthily among its members, and when we further realize that it expects us in every situation to be an honor to it. We have been made through the ministry of our gracious Lord, "Kings and priests unto his God and Father." If we believe this, and walk in the conscious light of the Lord, there cannot fail in time to be seen in us what was said of the brethren of Gideon: "Each one resembled the children of a king" (Judg. 8:18).

Victory over the Church's Foes

Among the spiritually significant stories of the Old Testament, there are none that contain deeper teaching for the individual overcomer and the whole militant Church of Christ than those of the outflow from the smitten rock at Rephidim and the ensuing battle with Amalek, recorded in the seventeenth chapter of the Book of Exodus. The lessons are so practical, they enter so deeply into the nature of the great conflict that is being fought in the heavenlies, they reveal so simply the technique of the warfare with our unseen foes, and they speak so confidently of complete and final victory, that there is little left to be said on the subject. There are other incidents in the Word which deal with differing phases of the same subject, and all are of value. But this gives the most comprehensive outline of the spiritual struggle involved, and it closes with a statement of the eternal purpose of God regarding the cooperation of His people in securing present and final triumph.

Our Heavenly Possessions

Israel had come into a great and priceless possession. Out of the smitten rock rivers of living water were flowing. They were a gift direct from the throne, abounding in life and blessing. They made possible the very existence of the people of Jehovah in the wilderness journey. The whole nation drank and was revived. There was no lack for either man or beast.

Rabbinical traditions speak of the streams following the host as it moved onward, the water flowing up the hills and down the valleys, and gathering in pools at the places of encampment. To these traditions the apostle refers (1 Cor. 10:4), when he speaks of the people drinking of "that spiritual rock that followed them; and that rock was Christ." In doing so, he does not give authority to the stories; his purpose is to direct attention to the Second Person of the Trinity who accompanied the nation, providing for its every need, and graciously protecting it in danger. The fact that a second time, towards the end of the wilderness wanderings, the rock was again smitten (Num. 20), indicates the necessity for a further supply of water, and reveals the falsity of the traditions.

For us there is a wealth of spiritual meaning in the record. "If any man thirst, let him come unto me, and drink," the Lord still cries unto His people. Christ at Calvary is the Smitten Rock of the New Testament Church. From His opened side flows the divine supply that satisfies every heart longing. So abundant is the fulness of the risen and living Lord, who dispenses that heavenly grace, that there is added to the invitation a wonderful promise: "He that believeth in me, out of his belly [from the depths of his inner life] shall flow rivers of living water." That is to say, the believer who abides at the Rock, and drinks continually of its outpouring, becomes himself a channel of blessing to other thirsty souls.

7

Victory over Spiritual Conflict

In the arid desert nothing is so vital as a supply of water. Sore conflicts frequently take place between the wandering tribes over the possession of a well or spring (see Gen. 26:18 ff.). It is not surprising, therefore, that the right of the people of Israel to the living streams of Rephidim was speedily contested. The fierce tribesmen of Amalek sought to drive them away, that they themselves might enjoy the abundance of this new oasis. Skilled warriors, trained in desert fighting, they were far more than a match for the recently liberated slaves of Pharaoh. Yet, untried as the Israelites were in warfare (Exod. 13:17), they must lay hold of spear and buckler, and defend their heaven-bestowed blessings. The battle in itself was a hopeless one for Israel. Wherever divine interference lessened, as the weary hands of Moses drooped, "Amalek prevailed." There was no natural ability in Israel to conquer; their victory came alone through the power of that Spiritual Rock that followed them.

One of the hard lessons that must be learned by every seeker after the deeper life in Christ is that each new appropriation of heavenly grace and knowledge brings him often into a more subtle conflict. In the early stages of the Christian life, when abounding peace and joy has come in to fill the heart, and the gladness of the Lord brightens all about him, his feet are "like hinds' feet," and he feels as if he were permanently established upon the spiritual "high places" (Hab. 3:19). But, ere long, he finds himself treading the Valley of Humiliation, where Apollyon must be faced, and passing thence to the dread experiences of the Valley of the Shadow of Death, where the evil ones press hard, and temptation assails with crushing force, and faith's contest with discouragement seems often a losing one.

Our Unseen Foes

As still further advancement in the knowledge of the Lord is given, through the opening of the eyes of his understanding, and he finds that he has been "blessed with every spiritual blessing in the heavenly places in Christ," there comes the startling realization that the very heavenly places, into which he has been introduced, are the habitat of the powers of darkness. His acceptance of his seat with Christ Jesus (Eph. 2:6) "far above all principality, and power, and might, and dominion," provides him with authority and power for full victory, so long as he maintains his place, wearing the defensive armor, and wielding the offensive weapons. But, unless at this stage of progress, there is received clear instruction as to the divine provision for overcoming, he is liable to spend many months, or even years, of fruitless struggle and defeat.

Nor can any believer escape this conflict, so long as he resolutely presses forward in the pursuit of true holiness and effective ministry. It is part of the training of the Lord's overcoming people. In the Kingdom Age, Christ has planned that they shall reign with Him from the heavenly places over the earth. It is consequently not strange that the principalities and powers, who are to be dispossessed of the seats of authority now occupied by themselves, should savagely resist their own displacement. These spiritual enemies oppose every forward step of the over-comer; they will seek to confuse his mind, sometimes drawing him into error, or into extravagance in doctrine. They may even attack him in body, or in circumstances, or through his family or his friends.

This has been their method in every age, as illustrated in the march of the hosts of Israel towards the Promised Land. Among the children of Israel the powers of darkness subtly introduced "many foolish and hurtful lusts"; they sought to seduce them by the incoming of idolatry and fornication from the nations around; they incited them to murmuring and distrust of the providence of Jehovah; or they openly and fiercely attacked them, as through the Amalekites. In the same manner today, by both inward and outward means, "the wiles of the devil" are directed to the rendering fruitless of the life and service of the individual Christian and of the aggressive church.

Many an earnest pastor weeps before the Lord because of coldness or disunion in his congregation. The successful evangelist is disturbed by some deadening influence creeping into the atmosphere of his meetings, by which his liberty of spirit is hampered, and by which souls are hindered from coming to the Savior. In many cases prayer does not seem to touch the difficulty, even when long continued. Nay, even prayer itself seems to be lifeless, and God afar off. At times the enemy strikes back swiftly when some special effort is aimed against him. Workers break down, sickness weakens the frame, spiritual purpose slackens, and discouragement throws a pall of darkness that depresses every effort for the Lord. Such experiences are far from uncommon, as many will testify.

The Authority of the Rod

What is the significance of the Rod as it appears in the ministry of Moses? The usual interpretation is that it symbolizes prayer. But there is no mention of prayer in the incident before us, and in a somewhat similar case (Exod. 14:15 ff.), the Lawgiver is sharply told that the time is past for calling on God, and that definite action is needed. There is a richer and more powerful meaning: *the rod symbolizes the authority of God committed to human hands.* By it the holder is made a co-ruler with his Lord, sharing His throne-power, and reigning with Him.

It is a vision that staggers the faith of many. But it is a scriptural revelation of divine truth, that is repeated in many places and in many forms. The overcoming saint is made a king and priest unto God (Rev. 1:6), that he may reign on the earth (Rev. 5:10). He is given authority over the nations (Rev. 2:26 ff.), cooperating with the risen Christ. He sits with the exalted Lord in the heavenly places (Eph. 1:20), which is the center of the authority of the universe. In this position of privilege he is enthroned with Christ "far above all principality, and power, and might and dominion, and every name that is named, not only in this age, but also in that which is to come."

This is meant to be a present experience of faith, though its full development will be reached in the age which is before us. Let us not dishonor the Word of God that reveals these things, by the unbelieving attitude that it means less than it has clearly stated.

All through the day, "until the going down of the sun," Moses held out the rod over the valley in which Israel strove with Amalek. Was he praying? There is little doubt that his heart was lifted to God in unceasing supplication for the untrained soldiers of his people. But his holding out of the rod was a demonstration of the authority committed to him over the unseen forces which drove forward the Amalekites, and which operate behind every battle (see Dan. 10:13, 20). Not in the visible, but in the invisible, lies the secret of success or failure. Over the spirit-foes of Israel, which sought to thwart the purpose of God, and to hold back His people from the land of their inheritance, Moses exercised the authority vested in him as the representative of Jehovah. By his sustained resistance to these mighty principalities and powers, their ability to aid the Amalekites was nullified. And, as the sun went down, the beaten tribesmen suddenly withdrew.

The principle holds in every conflict between the people of God and their enemies. Where redeemed man is concerned, the Father calls him into a ministry of authority with His Son, the rightful Ruler of earth. In the Old Testament, some remarkable instances occur, such as that of Joshua at Ajalon (Josh. 10:12), or that of Elijah (1 Kings 17:1), where the prophet boldly declared that "there shall not be dew or rain these years, but *according to my word.*" In those past ages, however, the authority was limited to a few select souls, upon whom the Spirit came for special ministries. But the New Testament saints of the heavenly places include all who are raised up with Christ, and who have accepted the death of the cross, and the burial of the tomb, that they may attain unto the resurrection of which Paul speaks (Phil. 3:11). For them there is a fellowship with the Risen Christ in a larger sense than others know. To them the powers of darkness yield wherever their authority is exerted.

The Hand Upon the Throne

"Jehovah hath sworn," reads the Revised

Version, "Jehovah will have war with Amalek from generation to generation." The first clause is not correctly translated. "A hand is lifted up upon the throne of Jehovah," the Hebrew reads. The lifting up of the hand is a form of affirmation or oath, and from this comes the rendering, "Jehovah hath sworn." The meaning is to be found in the action of Moses. Lifting up his hand holding the rod, he took authority in the name of Jehovah over the foes of God's people. In his capacity as the representative of Jehovah he was exerting the authority of the throne when he lifted up his hand. It was a declaration of divine judgment to be executed upon Amalek and upon the demon-powers who energized those cruel warriors in their enmity against Israel.

So, today, every consecrated hand that lifts the rod of the authority of the Lord against the unseen powers of darkness is directing the throne-power of Christ against Satan and his hosts in a battle that will last until "the going down of the sun," that is, until life's day is ended. Paul prayed (Eph. 1:17) that "The Spirit of wisdom and revelation in the knowledge of him [Christ]" might be granted to the saints to whom he wrote. Thus would the eyes of their understanding be opened to see their full relationship to the risen and exalted Christ.